INSPIRATIONAL FOOTBALL STORIES

FOR YOUNG CHAMPIONS

JACK GOLDER

CONTENTS

"The more difficult the victory,
the greater the happiness in winning."

—Pelé

Some people say football is "JUST A GAME!"

But if you've ever screamed when your team scored, stayed up too late playing FIFA, or practiced that one move over and over, you already know the truth:

Football is more than a sport. It's a way of life.

Every in this book legend started somewhere ordinary. None of them were "supposed to make it". All of them found a way.

This book is about REAL MOMENTS. Moments when everything came down to a single decision:
Keep going? Or give up?

Champions are made on days when it's tough, but show up anyway.
Every kick. Every tackle. Every goal.
Every moment on the pitch tells a story.
Every champion was once just a kid with a ball.

If they made it. So can you.

THE BOY WHO OUTRAN THE ODDS

Boots blurred across the grass and Alphonso was already gone.

"Davies on the left wing again, look at that pace!" shouted the commentator.

The clock read 67 minutes. Bayern Munich led 5–2, but he wasn't finished. He tore down the flank, one defender, two, three, gone.

"He's still going! He's still going!"

Then came Semedo. Alphonso dropped his shoulder, twisted, and sent him spinning. The crowd gasped.

"No way..." someone whispered in disbelief.

Davies cut inside, whipped the ball across the box. Kimmich timed it perfectly and... **"GOAL!"**

The stadium erupted. Alphonso threw up his hands, laughing as his teammates surrounded him.

As he looked up toward the sky, the roar of the crowd faded and his mind drifted back in time.

The stadium lights reminded him of the harsh sun that beat down on the refugee camp where he was born.

His parents had fled the war in Liberia with almost nothing. The camp was crowded and dusty. Some nights, the sound of crying mixed with the crickets. Alphonso would stare at the stars and wonder what was waiting beyond the fence.

His family made it safely to Canada when Alphonso was five. The snow was strange at first, the air so cold it burned his nose. But after everything he'd been through, the cold didn't scare him. It meant safety.

Some days at school, he didn't understand a word anyone said. He was shy and quiet most of the time, but the moment a ball rolled his way, he came to life.

By ten, he joined a community program called Free Footie, which helped kids who couldn't afford gear or travel fees. The rules were simple: no money, no pressure, just football.

He showed up in shoes too big for him. Still outran everyone.

When he was thirteen, Alphonso started attending youth team tryouts. Some coaches shook their heads when they saw him.

He'd get crushed in real competition, they said.

One evaluator even pulled his parents aside. "Maybe focus on school instead. Football might not work out."

Alphonso heard it all. Then he went back to training.

Every morning before school, he ran. Every evening after homework, he ran. When winter made the field too icy, he trained inside. He wasn't just proving the doubters wrong. He was proving himself right.

Coaches at Free Footie saw it. Every mistake became a lesson, every setback a reason to train harder.

Fun fact 🎮

> Alphonso Davies streams video games like FIFA and Call of Duty for fans in his spare time.

When others stopped to rest, he ran one more sprint.

He was learning one of football's biggest lessons: your circumstances don't decide your limits, your effort does.

At fourteen, scouts from the Vancouver Whitecaps noticed something different about Alphonso. He didn't just play fast, he thought fast.

At fifteen, he became the second-youngest player in MLS history.

His first season wasn't perfect. He made mistakes, lost the ball, mistimed his runs. Fans noticed.

The criticism came fast and furious.

After one tough match, a headline read:

"Is Davies Ready for This Level?"

So he did what winners do. He printed the headline and stuck it on his wall so he could see it every night before bed, every morning before training.

He turned their criticism into fuel. And it worked.

One night, his coach said, "Phonzie, you're not just fast, you make people believe."

He never forgot that.

By 2018, Bayern Munich came calling: a €13 million transfer, a record for MLS.

At nineteen, Alphonso lifted three trophies in one season: the Champions League, the Bundesliga, and the German Cup.

It was the kind of season most players only dream about. The roar of the crowd snapped him back to the present.

That assist became one of the most replayed plays in Champions League history.

Alphonso looked toward the bench where younger players watched. He remembered being the kid with shoes too big, wondering if he'd ever belong.Now he knew the truth: Speed gets you noticed. Heart keeps you going.

After the match, Alphonso looked at the younger players on the bench. He remembered what it felt like to be doubted.

If he could tell them one thing, it would be this:

Your circumstances are your starting point, not your limit.

ALPHONSO BY THE NUMBERS

- 15 years old as the second-youngest player in MLS history
- 19 years old when he won the continental treble with Bayern Munich.
- 150+ matches played for Bayern Munich before turning 23

Think like Alphonso...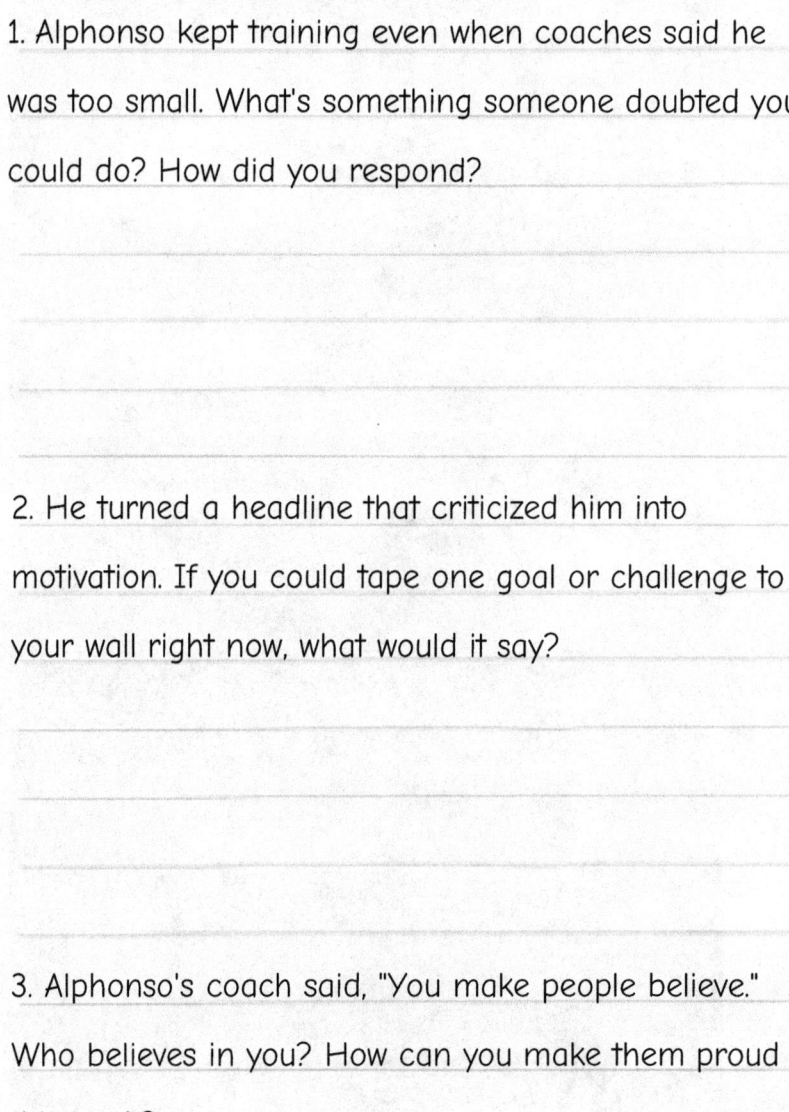

1. Alphonso kept training even when coaches said he was too small. What's something someone doubted you could do? How did you respond?

_____

_____

_____

2. He turned a headline that criticized him into motivation. If you could tape one goal or challenge to your wall right now, what would it say?

_____

_____

_____

3. Alphonso's coach said, "You make people believe." Who believes in you? How can you make them proud this week?

_____

_____

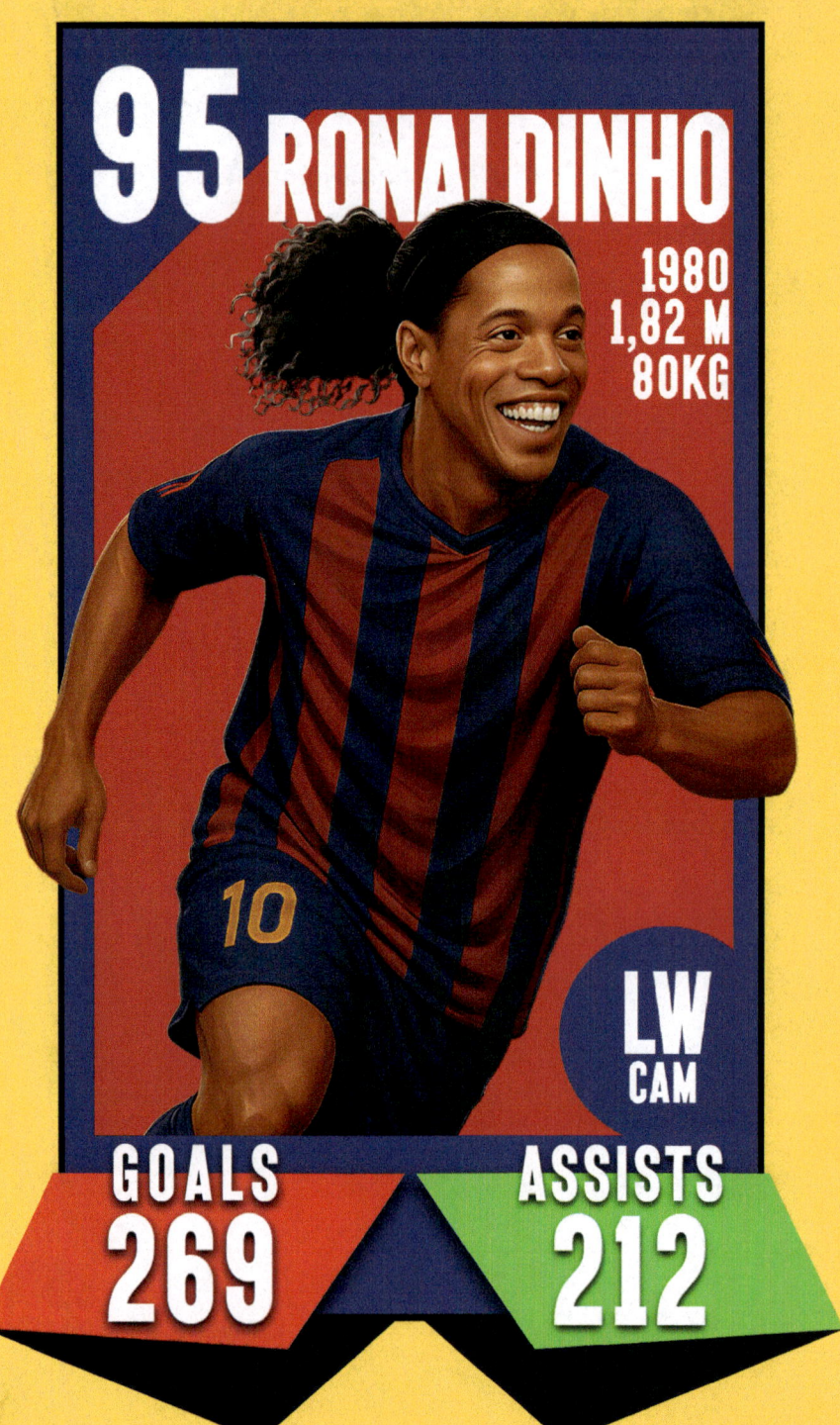

THE JOY OF FOOTBALL

What if football was a song? What if every touch, every turn, every laugh became part of its rhythm?

That's how Ronaldinho played, as if the game itself was music only he could hear.

Crowds roared as the ball danced at his feet, and when he scored, people didn't just cheer. They smiled.

He played with the same freedom no matter the pitch, even when the field was just a patch of dirt behind his house in Porto Alegre, Brazil.

In their small wooden house, football was more than a game. It was the family language.

His father worked nights at the Grêmio stadium. His brother played for the team. And Ronaldinho practiced with whoever he could, even his dog,

Bombom, the most loyal (and laziest) defender on the street.

When his father came home, tired but smiling, he'd always say the same thing:

"Play with joy, son. Always play with joy."

Every step he took as a professional echoed his father's philosophy: Joy before fear. Creativity before caution.

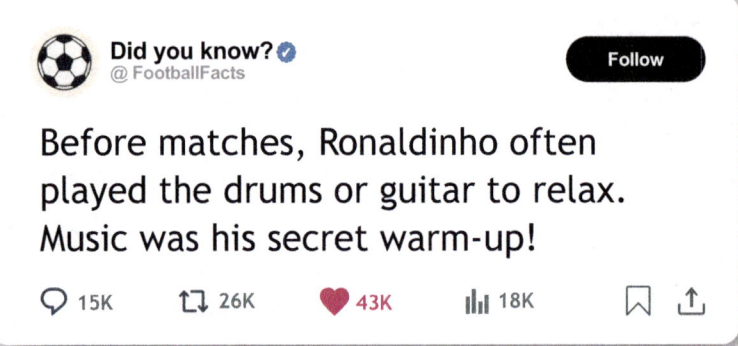

By eighteen, he was playing for his hometown club, Grêmio, dribbling past grown men as if gravity didn't apply to him.

Fans would arrive early just to watch his warm-ups. He'd juggle the ball on his neck, drop it to his heel, flick it over his head, and land it perfectly on his chest without breaking rhythm.

He made football look like magic because, for him, it was.

After leaving Grêmio for Paris Saint-Germain, Ronaldinho's magic only grew brighter.

He missed home. He didn't speak a word of French. And French newspapers weren't kind.

"He smiles too much," one sports writer complained. "Football is serious business."

"A waste of money," another headline read.

His new teammates didn't pass to him at first. They thought his tricks were selfish, that he cared more about looking good than winning.

But once the whistle blew, the language didn't matter.

The ball did the talking, and it left everyone speechless.

In 2002, wearing Brazil's blue kit, Ronaldinho lined up for a free kick against England in the World Cup quarterfinals.

Forty yards out.

Everyone expected a pass.

He smiled, ran up, and chipped the ball high into the air.

England's goalkeeper, David Seaman, stepped forward. The ball kept rising. Then it dipped. **GOAL.**

Brazil went on to win their fifth World Cup, and Ronaldinho's name became a promise: that anything can happen when you play with freedom.

When Barcelona signed him in 2003, the club was broken.

They had finished sixth the previous season. The fans were furious. The team was €180 million in debt. Morale was at rock bottom.

Critics shook their heads. "One player can't save a sinking ship."

Ronaldinho's solution to Barcelona's crisis was simple: he played as if the scoreboard didn't exist and the crowd was his family.

Every match became a highlight reel. Every touch looked effortless. Every goal came with a grin.

Joy, it turned out, was contagious.

By 2004 and 2005, he was crowned FIFA World Player of the Year. In 2005, he also won the Ballon d'Or, the most prestigious individual award in football.

The following season, he led Barcelona to the Champions League title, their first in fourteen years.

Did you know?

Fans call him O Mago which means "The Magician" in Portugese.

One night in Madrid, playing against Real, Barcelona's fiercest rival, Ronaldinho scored two goals so beautiful that even the rival fans stood and applauded.

Eighty thousand people.

Wearing white.

Clapping for the player in blue and red.

It had only happened once before in the stadium's history. That's what joy does.

It doesn't just win games. It wins hearts.

Fame came and went. Trophies gathered dust. Injuries slowed him down.

But one thing never left him: that smile.

Because Ronaldinho's real gift wasn't goals or tricks.

It was the reminder that football, like life, is supposed to be played with joy.

When you play with happiness, you don't just win games. You light up the world.

Today, when young players ask him for advice, Ronaldinho says the same thing his father told him:

"Play with joy. Always."

But here's what he learned that he wants YOU to know:

Joy isn't something you wait to feel. It's something you choose.

You choose it when you're nervous before a big game.

You choose it when you miss a shot.

You choose it when someone says you're not good enough.

The question isn't whether you CAN play with joy.

The question is: _Will you?_

Next time you step on the pitch, before the whistle blows, smile. Choose joy and see what happens.

RONALDINHO'S JOY WARM-UP

Before practice or a game, try this 3-minute routine:

1. **Smile Check:** Force yourself to smile for 10 seconds. (Studies show smiling reduces nerves, even fake smiles!)

2. **Juggle for Fun**: Juggle the ball 20 times, trying tricks you've never done. Don't count mistakes. Just play.

3. **Memory Moment**: Remember your favorite goal or save. Replay it in your mind like a highlight reel.

Ronaldinho did this before every match. He said:
"If I'm not enjoying the warm-up,
I won't enjoy the game."

THE POWER OF DISCIPLINE

Silence filled the locker room.

Atlético Madrid had just lost another match. Some players kicked the floor in frustration, others stared blankly at the ground.

Then Diego Simeone stepped into the doorway, hands in his pockets. Heads lifted.

He spoke with calm certainty. "We keep fighting. We keep believing. Order, effort, team. Always."

That moment said everything about El Cholo.

The nickname was born years before the suit, back when his dreams were bigger than the fields he played on.

As a kid, Diego trained like every practice was a final. He tied his boots tighter than anyone else, chasing every ball as if it carried his dream inside it.

One day, after a muddy training session, his coach shook his head and laughed. "You're not just Diego," he said. "You're El Cholo."

Diego grinned. He liked the sound of that.

In Argentina, El Cholo means The Street Fighter. The one who gives everything, always.

The name stuck, and so did the spirit.

But not everyone believed in the street fighter.

When Diego was 14, a scout from River Plate watched him play and shook his head. "Too aggressive," the scout said. "He'll never control his temper." Diego heard those words. He didn't argue.

He just trained harder, learning to channel fire into focus.

From that day on, he played every match like it was his first and his last, with a fire that never went out.

That spirit carried him everywhere: from Vélez Sarsfield to Atlético Madrid, Inter Milan, and Lazio, winning trophies in every country. For Argentina, he lifted two Copa América titles and earned 106 caps, a midfielder driven by pure will.

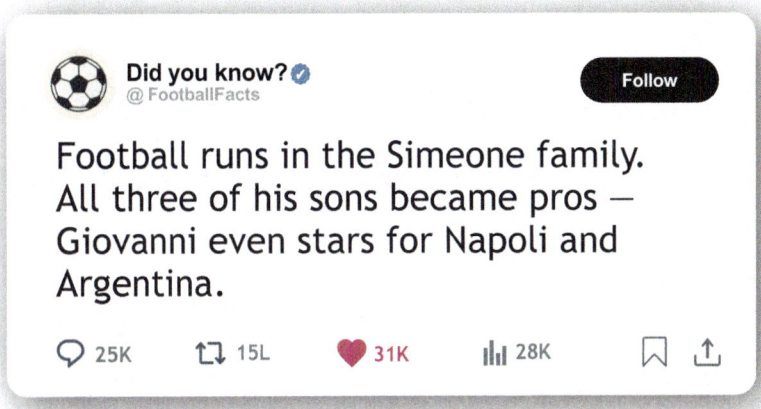

Did you know? ✔
@ FootballFacts

Follow

Football runs in the Simeone family. All three of his sons became pros — Giovanni even stars for Napoli and Argentina.

💬 25K   🔁 15L   ❤️ 31K   📊 28K   🔖 ⬆️

Even near the end of his playing days, Diego was already thinking like a coach.

He could never sit still on the bench, pointing, clapping, shouting instructions as if he were guiding an invisible team on the field.

Teammates laughed and called him "the captain from the sidelines."

One afternoon after training, a director asked, "If you were in charge, what would you change?"

Diego smiled, tapped the badge on his chest, and said, "Order. Effort. Team."

When he finally hung up his boots, he didn't walk away from football. He simply changed uniform.

His teammates' jokes became reality. Diego coached in Argentina and Italy for five years, learning his craft at Racing, River Plate, and San Lorenzo. He made mistakes, studied tactics, and sharpened his philosophy.

Then in 2011, Atlético Madrid called him home, this time as their coach.

Diego walked into the dressing room in a black suit carrying an Atlético Madrid shirt. He placed it carefully on a chair.

"This is not cloth," he said. "It is a promise."

Training changed the very next morning.

Forwards learned to tackle. Defenders learned to score.

Everyone ran, everyone helped the teammate beside them.

He taught them that defending was bravery, that patience was power, and that belief was something you practiced every single day.

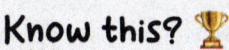

Know this? 🏆

By December 2021, Simeone had more wins than any coach in Atletico's history. 326 victories in 551 matches!

Truth is, the team was struggling. Barcelona and

Real Madrid seemed untouchable, winning nearly every trophy for years.

But Simeone saw something others didn't. Little by little, the team grew stronger.

Before the final match of the 2014 season, a sports journalist asked Simeone if he really believed Atlético could dethrone Barcelona.

Diego smiled. "Watch us," he said. That weekend, Atlético drew 1-1 at Camp Nou. It was just enough to claim the title.

And then, in 2014, the impossible happened.

Atlético Madrid won La Liga, breaking the long dominance of Barcelona and Real Madrid.

Players collapsed on the pitch, exhausted and in tears. Simeone clenched his fists and smiled. He had built champions through unity, order, and trust.

In 2021, he did it again. Proof that belief is not luck, it's a way of life. His philosophy, Cholismo, became legendary. It's a way of living that means: fight with heart, stay humble, and trust your team.

Under his leadership, Atlético won two La Liga titles, two Europa Leagues, and reached two Champions League finals.

After more than 600 matches in charge, Simeone stands among football's most respected managers, admired even by rivals for building teams that never stop running or believing.

The "Cholismo" Philosophy

Simeone built champions through discipline and belief. Use these five rules to bring that same energy to your game.

1. **Be early, be ready** → Beat the coach to the pitch. Be ready before everyone else.

2. **Do your job, lift the team** → Handle your position, then support the one beside you.

3. **Celebrate tackles, not only goals** → Defense is courage. Effort earns respect

4. **Learn from every match** → Whether you win or lose, keep training, keep learning, keep growing.

5. **Hand on badge, make a vow** → Order. Effort. Team. Every single day.

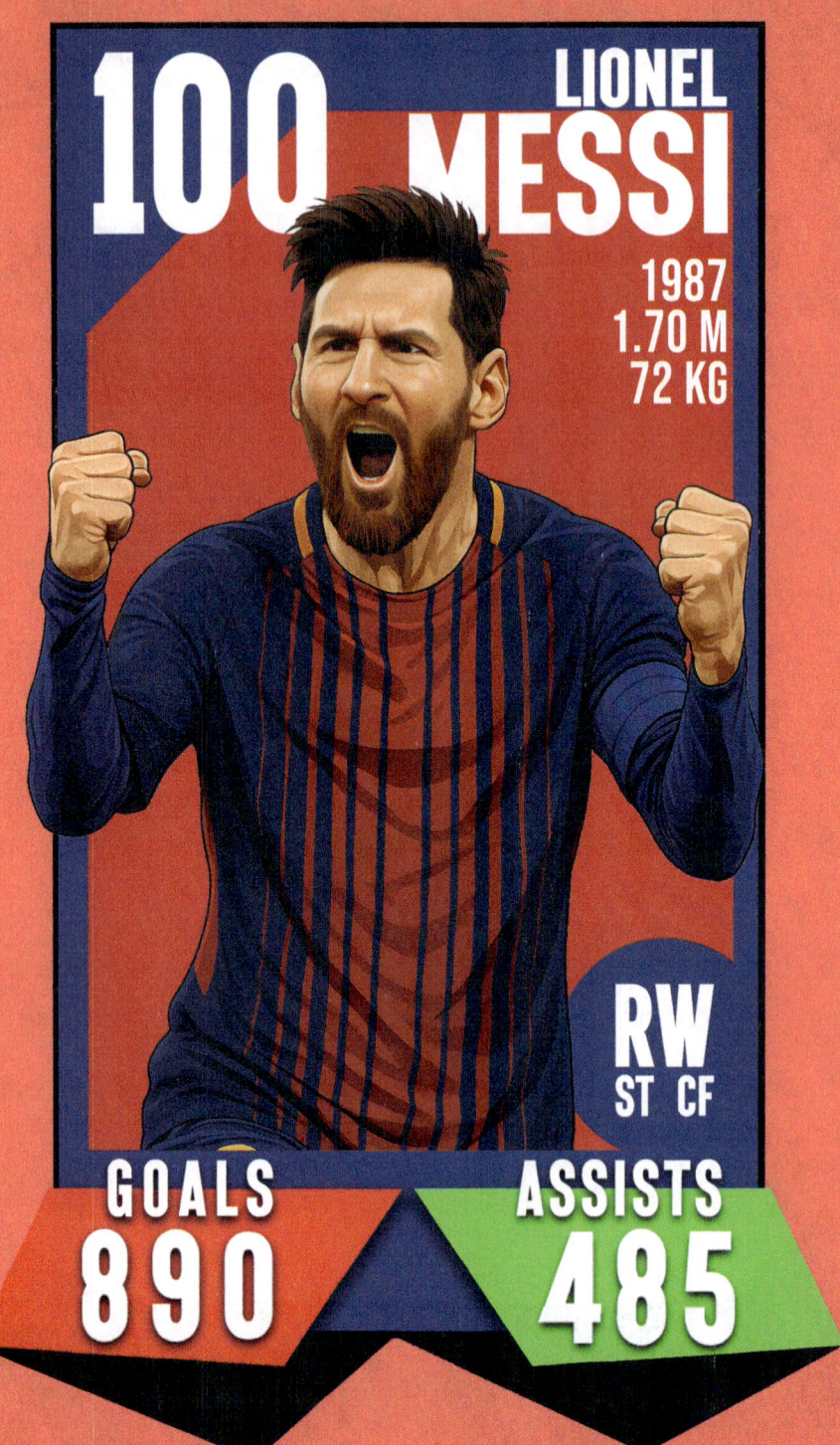

THE TINY GIANT

Three football legends sat in a tennis club in Barcelona.

No, this isn't the start of a bad joke. It's the moment that changed football forever.

Horacio Gaggioli sighed. "Carles, are your Barça people coming or what?"

Carles Rexach just smiled, grabbed a napkin, and began to write. His eyes kept drifting to the quiet boy at the end of the table.

He signed, then slid the napkin across. "There," he said softly. "Football history on paper."

The boy read: *"In Barcelona, on December 14, 2000, I, Carles Rexach, agree to sign Lionel Messi..."*

A smile spread across his face, his hands trembling just a little.

A year later, Lionel arrived at La Masia with a backpack, a football, and a promise to himself.

He was smaller than everyone, not just other kids his age, but even boys two years younger than him. At 11, he looked 8. His kit hung loose and his socks almost met his shorts.

Ever heard this? ⚡

> Messi's nickname is "La Pulga" (The Flea) because of his tiny size and quick movements. 🤩

Back home in Argentina, doctors had delivered hard news. He had a condition called growth hormone deficiency.

The solution was small injections into his legs. Every night.

The needle stung. Some nights Leo cried quietly, hoping his parents wouldn't hear. His father gave him the injections every night, a painful routine that lasted for years.

Some weeks, his legs ached so badly he could barely train. Doctors warned that without the treatment, he might never grow enough to chase his dream.

When he arrived at Barcelona, some of the older academy boys laughed.

"You're too small to make it here," one said, smirking. "Barcelona will send you home in a month."

MESSI BY THE NUMBERS

- **8 Ballon d'Ors:** Most in football history (2009, 2010, 2011, 2012, 2015, 2019, 2021, 2023)

- **672 goals for Barcelona:** All-time leading scorer for one club in football history

- **Over 820 career goals:** Across club and country

- **35 trophies with Barcelona:** Including 10 La Liga titles and 4 Champions League trophies

When others saw how small he was, they made the mistake of underestimating him.

A heartbeat later, he was gone and they could only watch, mouths wide open, as the net shook behind them.

Did you know? ✔
@ FootballFacts

Follow

In 2012, Messi broke the previous world record for most goals in a calendar year, scoring a staggering 91 goals! 😮

💬 27K   🔁 21K   ❤️ 59K   📊 35K   🔖 ⬆️

He wore number 30 at first, the digits huge on a shirt that hung loose on his small frame.

It was a start. But Leo wanted the number 10.

In Argentina, number 10 is sacred. It was the number of Maradona, the hero every kid wanted to be.

For Leo, it was a symbol of creativity, courage, and the responsibility to lift an entire team.

Then came his debut.

Seventeen years old. The stage set. The Camp Nou buzzing.

When Leo touched the ball for the first time, the rhythm of the game changed.

He twisted past defenders twice his size as if gravity didn't apply to him. His feet moved so fast the ball looked glued to his boots.

A few years later, Barcelona gave him the number 10 jersey, the very number he had dreamed of as a kid.

Leo just smiled, nodded, and pulled it over his head.

To him, it wasn't about fame or status. It was about trust.

The club trusting him to carry the weight of a team.

The fans trusting him to bring the magic back.

And Leo did, with goals, assists and moments that made the world hold its breath.

Then came November 29, 2010. One of the biggest games in football history.

Barcelona vs Real Madrid. El Clásico.

The tension was thick. Both teams wanted to prove they were the best.

From the first whistle, Barcelona dominated.

Messi didn't just play. He ran the game.

Every pass felt like magic. Every movement opened space. Madrid's defenders chased shadows, desperate to keep up.

By the time the final whistle blew, the scoreboard read:

Barcelona 5 – Real Madrid 0

Camp Nou shook with noise. Fans chanted "Olé!" with every Barcelona touch.

Cristiano Ronaldo threw his arms up in frustration.

Mourinho stood on the sideline, hands over his face, helpless.

Messi didn't even score that night, but he made the whole game dance around him.

But football hadn't given him everything yet. There was one dream still out of reach, and it was breaking his heart.

Winning with Argentina.

The 2014 World Cup final. Lost 1-0 to Germany

The 2015 Copa América final. Lost 4-1 to Chile.

The 2016 Copa América final. Lost 4-2 to Chile.

By the third loss, something broke.

Leo stood on the pitch, tears streaming down his face.

He'd been given Argentina's sacred number 10. The number of legends. The number that carried the weight of a nation's hopes.

And he felt like he'd let them all down.

So he made a decision that shocked the world.

He announced his retirement that night, but Argentina wouldn't let him go.

Within weeks, fans held signs: "Don't leave us, Leo." Teammates called every day. The whole country told him the same thing: "We need you."

Less than two months later, he came back.

Then, five years later, in 2021, he finally lifted the Copa América trophy. And in 2022, at age 35, he led Argentina to World Cup glory.

When people asked Leo how he did it, he always answered the same way:

"Work hard. Enjoy the game. Get better every day."

The magic on match day didn't come from talent alone. It came from years of quiet mornings and endless practice.

He worked through pain others couldn't handle. The injections. The doubt. The losses. He never looked for shortcuts. But that's how champions are made.

Messi's career wasn't built on one magical moment.It was built on thousands of small moments, early morning practices, extra hours in the gym, quiet nights with a ball at his feet.

He didn't wait for talent to carry him. He worked when no one was watching.

Here's what Messi would tell you:

"The difference between dreaming and achieving is what you do when no one's looking. Every touch matters. Every practice counts."

MESSI'S "CLOSE CONTROL" DRILL

What you need: One ball and a small space.

The Drill:

- Place the ball between your feet
- Using only small touches with the inside of your feet, move the ball in a tight circle around you
- Switch directions every 10 touches
- Keep the ball as close as possible—imagine you're protecting it from defenders
- Practice for 5 minutes every day

Why it works:

Messi's superpower lies on control. He twists and turns with the ball glued to his feet, a skill forged by hours of childhood practice.

85

JAMIE
VARDY

1987
1.79 M
74 KG

ST

GOALS
244

ASSISTS
89

THE UNSTOPPABLE UNDERDOG

The whistle blew and Jamie grinned.

Funny how that sound used to mean the end of another factory shift.

Back then, his boots weren't covered in grass. They were tucked under a workbench beside the smell of glue and metal.

Machines hissed and clanked as Jamie bent over another mold, shaping braces for tired legs. His own legs ached too, but for a different reason.

They wanted to run.

He'd glance at the clock. 4:57 p.m. Almost time.

"Off to training again?" a coworker teased.

Jamie wiped his hands and smiled. "Every night."

By 6 o'clock he was on a muddy pitch at Stocksbridge Park Steels. No floodlights. No fancy locker rooms. Just cold wind, heavy boots, and a handful of mates chasing the same dream.

Thirty pounds a week. That was his pay.

But every sprint, every slide tackle, every goal felt like a small step toward something bigger.

Even when the finish line was nowhere in sight, he kept running toward it.

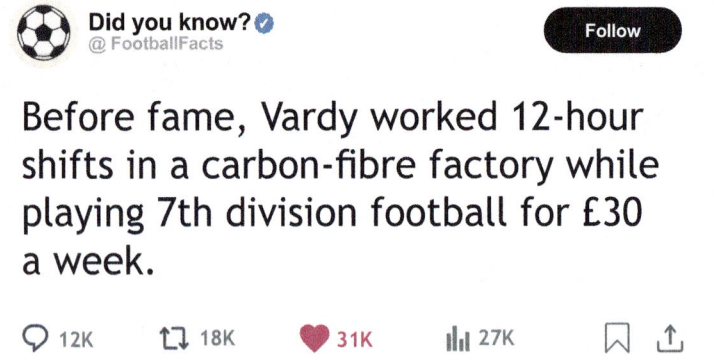

When Jamie was 16, Sheffield Wednesday let him go.

No explanation. No second chance. Just a letter saying they were releasing him from the academy.

Jamie's dad drove him home in silence.

In his room that night, Jamie stared at his boots in the corner. Maybe they were right. Maybe he wasn't meant for this.

Then he laced them up anyway.

Each rejection became fuel. Each "no" made his legs burn faster.

For eight years, Jamie played in the seventh and eighth tiers of English football. Muddy pitches. Broken changing rooms. Crowds of two hundred people.

Most players would have quit. Jamie just ran harder.

By 24, Jamie got a chance at Halifax Town, then Fleetwood Town, where he scored thirty-one goals in one season.

Scouts started whispering his name.

In 2012, Leicester City took a wild gamble and paid £1 million for a non-league player. It was almost unheard of.

The headlines weren't kind.

"Non-league gamble." "Wasted million."

"He'll be gone by Christmas."

Even some Leicester fans doubted.

Jamie didn't read the papers. He just did what he always did. He ran like he was still chasing his dream through the mud, pressing defenders and sprinting with a fire in his heart.

Then came 2015.

Leicester City were supposed to get relegated. Instead, something impossible started happening.

Jamie scored. Then he scored again. And again.

Week after week, he found the net. The world started counting.

One goal. Two. Five. Eight. Ten.

On November 28, 2015, he scored his 11th goal in 11 straight matches, breaking Ruud van Nistelrooy's Premier League record.

The goal came against Manchester United. The team that represented everything he'd once dreamed of becoming.

When the ball hit the net, Jamie didn't celebrate like a superstar. He celebrated like a factory worker who'd never forgotten where he came from.

People said Leicester City couldn't win the league.

Five thousand to one odds, they said. The same odds as finding Elvis alive or seeing the Loch Ness Monster.

But Jamie didn't care about the odds.

Can you believe this? 🤔

According to one report, Vardy used vodka mixed with Skittles during recovery!

By May, Leicester were champions of England for the first time in 132 years.

The factory worker had become a football king.

Jamie didn't stop there.

In 2020, at 33 years old, he became the oldest player ever to win the Premier League Golden Boot with 23 goals.

Players his age were retiring. Jamie was still outrunning defenders half his age.

Why? Because he never forgot the lesson from those cold nights at Stocksbridge Park Steels.

Success doesn't come looking for you.

You chase it.

Jamie learned that every mistake, every long day, every person who said "no" was part of the climb.

Real-life fairytales aren't written by luck. They're written with sweat, courage, and a heart that refuses to stop believing.

The factory worker became a champion because he made one choice, over and over: to keep running towards his dream.

Think like Jamie....

1. Jamie was rejected by Sheffield Wednesday at 16.
What rejection or disappointment have you faced?
How did it feel?

2. Jamie worked in a factory and trained every night,
even when exhausted. What could you do regularly
(even when tired) to chase your dream?

3. Who are YOUR doubters? How can you use their
doubt as fuel instead of letting it stop you?

THE SPECIAL ONE

Rain fell over the Estádio do Dragão in Portugal as José Mourinho stood on the touchline, hands in pockets, water dripping from his jacket.

His Porto team was facing giants—teams with more money, more stars, more history. Teams no one expected them to beat.

The crowd roared. The clock ticked. His players looked to the bench.

Mourinho simply nodded and said:

"We are not afraid. We are prepared."

Ninety minutes later, Porto were champions of Europe—and the world knew his name.

But before that moment, José Mourinho was far from being a champion.

He wasn't even a player.

José was born in Setúbal, Portugal. His father was a professional goalkeeper, and José grew up loving football.

He dreamed of playing professionally, just like his dad.

But injuries ended that dream early.

Some people said: "If you can't play, you can't coach."

José didn't argue.

He just found another way in.

When his playing career ended, José stayed close to the game. He learned languages—English, Spanish, Italian—and became a translator for one of the world's best coaches, Sir Bobby Robson.

His job was simple: turn English words into Portuguese, and Portuguese words into English.

But while José translated, he was also learning.

He studied how Sir Bobby built winning teams. He watched how players responded to different kinds of coaching. He asked questions after every training session.

Other translators went home after work.

José stayed late—watching video, memorizing

Mourinho once hid in a laundry basket to sneak into the dressing room during a UEFA ban, just so he could give his Chelsea team a pre-match talk.

patterns, taking notes in a small notebook he kept in his pocket.

He worked with Sir Bobby at Sporting Lisbon, then Porto, then Barcelona. For years, he stood on the sidelines, quiet and focused, learning from the best.

And the whole time, he was preparing for something bigger.

In 2002, José got his chance.

He was named head coach of FC Porto—a club that was struggling and had just finished third in the league. No one expected much. But Mourinho had a plan.

He studied every opponent for hours. He knew their strengths, their weaknesses, even which players got nervous under pressure.

He practiced specific situations with his team— what to do in the 90th minute when they were tired, what to do if they went down a goal, what to do if the referee made a bad call.

By the time Porto stepped onto the pitch, they weren't just ready. They were more prepared than anyone else.

Two years later, they won the UEFA Cup.

And then, in 2004, they did the impossible:

They won the Champions League—beating some of the richest, most famous teams in the world. When the final whistle blew, Mourinho sprinted down the touchline, arms spread wide, celebrating the moment that would change his life forever.

The translator had become a champion. That summer, one of the biggest clubs in the world came calling: Chelsea, in England.They hadn't won the league in fifty years.

In his first press conference, reporters asked José if he felt pressure.

He smiled and said:

"Please don't call me arrogant, but I'm not one of the bottle. I think I'm a special one."

MOURINHO BY THE NUMBERS

- 26 major trophies across 5 countries
- Won league titles in 4 different countries
- 2× Champions League winner
- 95 points with Chelsea 2004/05
- 100 points with Real Madrid 2011/12

The room went quiet. Some people laughed. Others thought he was cocky. But José wasn't bluffing.

He believed in his preparation. He believed in his method. And he believed his team could do something no Chelsea team had done in half a century.

One year later, Chelsea won the Premier League with a record 95 points. The "Special One" had done it again.

José Mourinho carried that same precision everywhere he went:

The Treble with Inter Milan in 2010 (league, cup, and Champions League in one season).

A 100-point season with Real Madrid in 2012—a La Liga record that still stands.

Europa League and League Cup double with Manchester United in 2017. His preparation bordered on obsession. He watched hours of video. He studied every opponent.

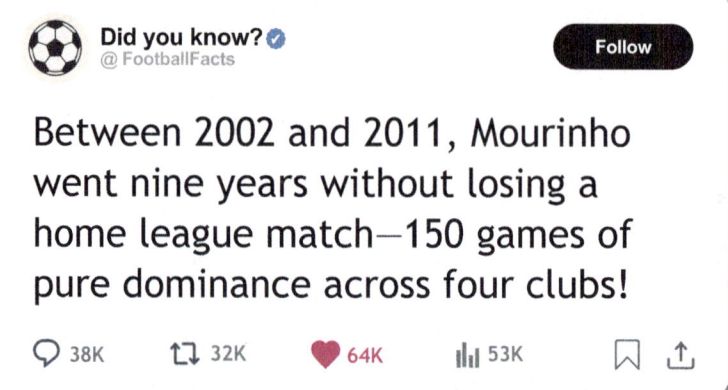

Did you know? ✔
@ FootballFacts

Follow

Between 2002 and 2011, Mourinho went nine years without losing a home league match—150 games of pure dominance across four clubs!

💬 38K   🔁 32K   ❤️ 64K   📊 53K   🔖   ⬆️

He remembered players' birthdays. He spotted injuries before doctors did. And he never asked his players to do anything he wouldn't demand of himself.

When critics doubted him, he smiled and got back to work. "These aren't trophies," he once said quietly. "They're the result of people working together."

José Mourinho proved that you don't need to be the fastest player or the biggest star. You don't even need to play to succeed in football.

What you need is preparation. You need to study harder than everyone else. You need to believe in your plan—even when others laugh. You need to pay attention when others think the work is boring.

And when your moment comes? You need to be ready.

The translator became a champion because he never stopped learning. He began on the sidelines and ended up shaping an era.

Your turn: What's one thing you can prepare for this week—before it happens?

THE POWER OF HARD WORK

Stockholm shook. November 19, 2013. Portugal needed a miracle to reach the World Cup.

The score: 2–2. Sweden charging forward. Noise like thunder rolling through the stadium. Then Cristiano Ronaldo burst into space—one touch to control, one strike to finish.

GOAL.

Hat-trick complete. Portugal 3–2 on aggregate. World Cup qualified. He stood still for a moment, chest heaving, eyes locked on the stands. A small nod that said: *This is why I train.*

The cheers faded in his mind, replaced by a voice from home—years ago, across the ocean.

"Cristiano! Dinner!"

A narrow street in Madeira, Portugal. Laughter echoing off stone walls. A ball bouncing between puddles.

"After this goal!" he shouted back, chasing the game like it was life itself. On that small island, footballs didn't just roll—they flew.

And young Cristiano chased them like his future depended on it.

He was thirteen, all elbows and energy, dribbling through winding alleys, dodging cars and puddles. Sometimes the ball was leather. Sometimes it was socks tied with string.

Then, at fifteen, everything stopped.

"You have tachycardia," the doctor said, looking at the test results. "Your heart beats irregularly. If you keep playing at this intensity, it could stop."

The words hung in the air like a death sentence.

For the first time in his life, Cristiano, the boy who lived to move, had to sit still.

No running. No training. No football.

Surgery or silence. Those were his options.

When the bandages finally came off and the doctor cleared him to play again, Cristiano returned to the pitch like someone reborn.

He had beaten his toughest opponent—his very own heart. But not everyone believed he'd make it.

At Sporting CP's academy in Lisbon, some coaches whispered: "Too flashy. Too much show. Not enough substance."

Teammates rolled their eyes when he did step-overs in training.

The Ronaldo Rule:

If you want to be better than everyone else, you have to practice more than everyone else. 💪

"Stop showing off," they'd say. "You're not Ronaldo. You're just Cristiano."

He heard them.

He didn't argue. He didn't quit.

Instead, he stayed after practice—two hours, three hours—working on his weaknesses.

Free kicks until his foot ached.

Sprints until his lungs burned.

Headers until the sun went down.

Did you know? ✔
@ FootballFacts

Follow

A bright, distant galaxy was dubbed "CR7" in reference to both Ronaldo's famous shirt number 7 and his superstar status in Portugal.

💬 40K   🔁 53K   ❤️ 72K   📊 49K

He'd stand in front of the mirror in the gym and practice his moves in slow motion, over and over, until they became automatic. The doubters thought he was wasting time. He was building a weapon.

August 2003. Sporting CP vs. Manchester United. A friendly match in Lisbon to open Sporting's new stadium. An 18-year-old Cristiano started on the right wing, wearing green and white. Early in the match, he received the ball near midfield.

He exploded forward—step-over left, step-over right—a burst of speed that left the first defender stumbling backward.

Then another defender came. Another step-over. Another burst.

The crowd gasped.

Manchester United's players looked at each other in disbelief.

By the end of the match, Sporting had won 3–1—and United's players couldn't stop talking about "the kid in green and white."

On the flight home, Rio Ferdinand grabbed manager Sir Alex Ferguson's arm: "Boss, we HAVE to sign that kid." Ferguson smiled. He'd already decided.

Weeks later, Cristiano Ronaldo signed with Manchester United—new club, new country, new number: 7. Same hunger.

July 10, 2016. Paris, France.

EURO 2016 Final. Portugal vs. France.

Portugal had never won a major tournament. Ever.

And Cristiano—their captain, their leader, their best player—was determined to change that.

But in the 25th minute, disaster struck.

A French player collided with Cristiano's knee. He crumpled to the ground, clutching his leg, face twisted in pain.

The stadium went silent.

He tried to keep playing. He limped back onto the pitch, gritting his teeth. He couldn't do it.

Tears streamed down his face as he was carried off on a stretcher, his dream slipping away.

But instead of sitting in the locker room feeling sorry for himself, Cristiano stood on the sideline—coaching, encouraging, shouting instructions, refusing to give up even when he couldn't play.

In extra time, his teammate Eder scored.

Portugal 1–0 France.

When the final whistle blew, Cristiano—still injured, still in pain—sprinted onto the pitch, jumping and shouting like he'd scored the goal himself.

Portugal's first major trophy. Ever.

Their captain had led them there—even from the sideline.

Cristiano Ronaldo went on to conquer everything:

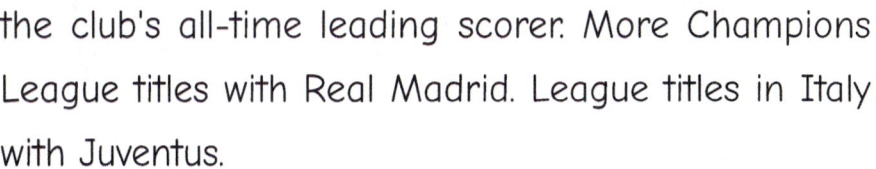

Premier League titles with Manchester United. Champions League glory in 2008. A record-breaking move to Real Madrid, where he became the club's all-time leading scorer. More Champions League titles with Real Madrid. League titles in Italy with Juventus.

But more than the trophies, more than the goals, more than the records— Cristiano Ronaldo rewrote what was possible through sheer will and relentless work.

He taught the world that greatness isn't talent, it's work.

It's staying when others leave. It's practicing your weaknesses until they become strengths. It's getting back up when your body says stop. It's leading even when you can't play.

The boy who almost lost his heartbeat became the player who never stopped fighting.

From a tiny island to the biggest stages in the world.

From "too flashy" to five-time world champion.

From doubted to unstoppable.

SIUUU!!

His signature celebration— a powerful jump, a mid-air twist, then landing with arms out, shouting "Siuuu!"—has become one of the most recognisable in football.

7

THE RONALDO "EXTRA HOUR"

Cristiano didn't just practice—he practiced after practice.

Here's what he did (and what you can do too):

1. Identify Your Weakness

What's the ONE skill you struggle with most?
For Ronaldo: weak foot shooting, heading, free kicks

2. Practice It When Your'e Already Tired

After regular practice, stay for 15-30 more minutes
Why? Because in real games, you're tired in the final
minutes, that's when you need your skills most

3. Make It Specific

Don't just "practice shooting". Practice shooting from the
EXACT spot you'll shoot from in games
Ronaldo practiced free kicks from every angle around the
box

4. Track Your Progress

Count: How many did you make out of 20 attempts?
Next time, try to beat that number.

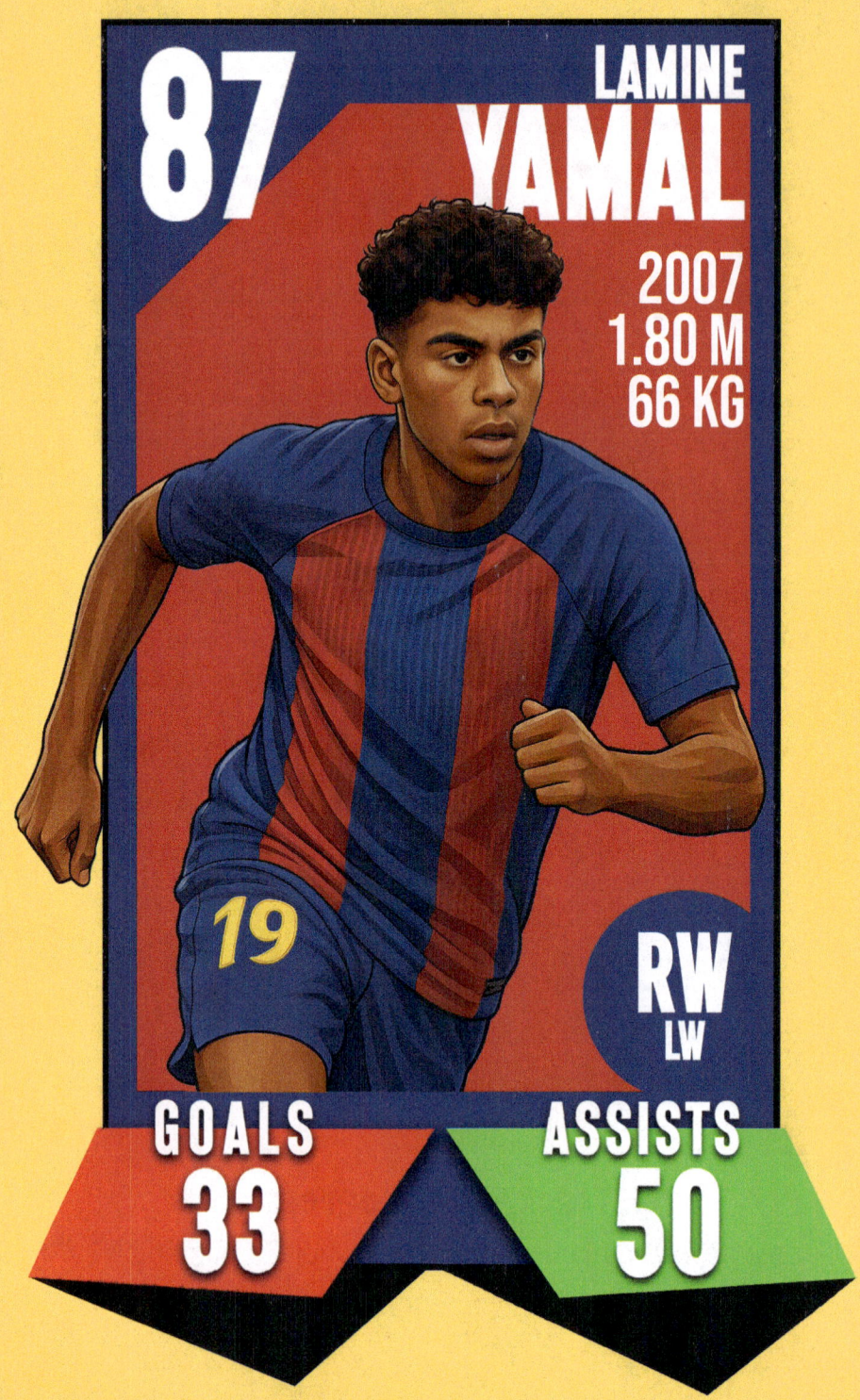

THE RISING STAR

The Camp Nou lights burned bright against the night sky. A roar rolled across the stands as a skinny 16-year-old stepped onto the pitch, his number 27 flashing under the floodlights.

"Go on, Lamine!" someone shouted from the bench.

The ball came to him—first touch, perfect. Second touch, a quick dribble past a defender twice his size. The crowd gasped.

Calm. Confident. Fearless.

Lamine Yamal, the youngest player ever to wear Barcelona's famous shirt, was already playing like he belonged.

Long before that night, Lamine kicked his first ball on the streets of Esplugues de Llobregat, just outside Barcelona.

Born in 2007 to a Moroccan father and Equatoguinean mother, he grew up with a mix of cultures, colors, and dreams.

Every evening after school, he'd challenge older kids to street matches. They were bigger. Faster. But Lamine had something they didn't: a first touch so soft the ball seemed to stick to his foot like glue.

"How do you do that?" one of the older boys asked.

Lamine shrugged. "I just talk to the ball until it listens."

He practiced barefoot in his garden for hours—left foot, right foot, tight spaces, quick turns—until the ball became an extension of himself.

At La Masia, Barça's world-famous academy, Lamine was always the youngest—sometimes by two or three years.

Some coaches whispered concerns. "Talented, yes. But is he ready for the pressure?"

One scout wrote in his evaluation report: "Exceptional talent, but mentally too young for first-team football. Needs 2-3 more years."

Lamine read it, smiled, and decided to prove them wrong in 2-3 months instead.

At 14, he was left out of a key youth tournament. The selection report was blunt: "Not ready for this level yet."

Pass the spark ✨

> Compliment a teammate's skill today. Champions lift others, not just trophies.

Instead of complaining, Lamine spent that week doing extra training sessions and watching videos of how Neymar and Ronaldinho used creativity to break down defenses.

He didn't argue with the doubters.

He just kept proving them wrong.

While other kids tried to copy Messi's dribbles or Ronaldo's celebrations, Lamine decided something different.

"I don't want to be the next anyone," he said. "I want to be me."

He studied the greats—but he didn't imitate them. He took what worked and mixed it with his own flair: cheeky nutmegs, no-look passes, calm decision-making under pressure.

While older players studied match tapes in slow motion, Lamine grew up watching highlight reels on TikTok and Instagram—learning to play with flair and fearlessness, not caution.

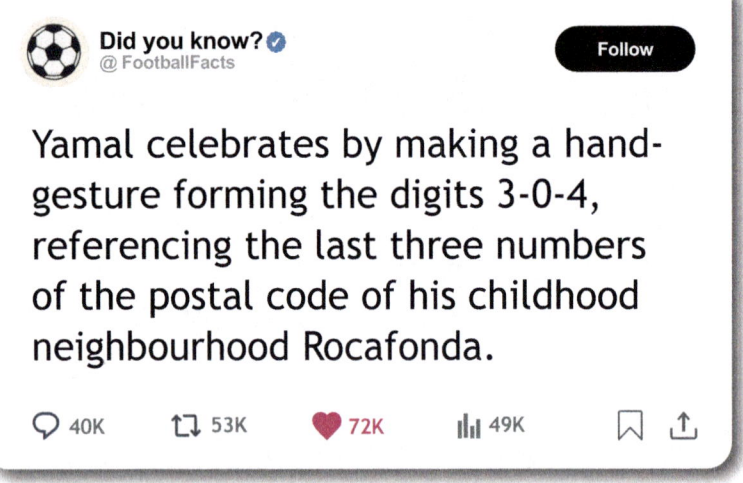

Did you know? ✔
@ FootballFacts

Follow

Yamal celebrates by making a hand-gesture forming the digits 3-0-4, referencing the last three numbers of the postal code of his childhood neighbourhood Rocafonda.

💬 40K   🔁 53K   ❤️ 72K   📊 49K

He wasn't trying to be perfect.

He was trying to be electric.

At 15 years old, he got a call most players only dream about—training with Barcelona's first team.

In that session, legends like Lewandowski and Pedri watched him glide past defenders with confidence that didn't match his age.

Coach Xavi Hernández just smiled. "This kid has ice in his veins."

On April 29, 2023, Lamine Yamal stepped onto the Camp Nou pitch as a substitute.

15 years and 290 days old.

The youngest player in FC Barcelona's history.

The crowd held its breath. Could he handle it?

Lamine touched the ball. A quick turn. A through pass that split two defenders. The stadium erupted.

Months later, he scored his first goal for Barcelona on September 8, 2023. Then, at 16 years and 57 days, he became Spain's youngest-ever goalscorer in a national team match.

Commentators shouted, "He's only sixteen!"

Lamine didn't celebrate wildly. He just grinned—calm as always—like it was just another day on the playground.

By the summer of 2024, Lamine Yamal wasn't just a prodigy anymore. He was Spain's secret weapon at the UEFA European Championship.

In the semifinal against France, Spain needed something special. The score was tied. The pressure was massive. Lamine received the ball 25 yards from goal. A defender rushed at him.

Most players would panic. Pass backward. Play it safe.

Not Lamine.

He took one touch to steady himself. Then he curled the ball with his left foot—bending it past the goalkeeper's outstretched hand and into the top corner.

GOAL. The stadium exploded. Teammates mobbed him.

The commentators screamed, "A SIXTEEN-YEAR-OLD JUST SCORED IN A EUROS SEMIFINAL!"

Lamine stayed calm. He pointed to the sky, smiled, and jogged back to the halfway line.

His message was clear: Talent has no age.

Spain went on to win the tournament, making Lamine the youngest player ever to win a European Championship.

Lamine Yamal didn't wait to be older, bigger, or "ready enough." He didn't wait for permission to be great. He trusted his game—and backed himself when others doubted.

Here's what Lamine would tell you:

"Don't wait for the perfect moment. Don't wait until you're older or more experienced. Your moment is now. The only question is: are you brave enough to take it?"

YOUR TURN:

What's one bold thing you've been afraid to try? What would happen if you tried it this week?

GREECE
2004 EURO WINNERS

THE INSIDE STORY

The stadium in Lisbon exploded with noise.

Greece, a team nobody believed in, had just beaten Portugal 1–0 in the Euro 2004 final. Angelos Charisteas rose high above the defenders, heading the ball into the net.

The underdogs were champions of Europe.

Before the tournament started, the jokes came fast and cruel.

Bookmakers gave Greece 150-to-1 odds to win the tournament. These were the same odds you'd get betting on a last-place team winning the league.

Greece had never won a match at a major tournament before 2004. Not one. Their squad was filled mostly with players from mid-table clubs across Europe. No superstars. No household names.

Even their own fans traveled to Portugal expecting sun and beaches, not silverware.

Their manager, Otto Rehhagel, was a 65-year-old German who had never won a major international tournament. When reporters asked about his tactics, he smiled.

Did you know? ✓
@ FootballFacts

Follow

Otto Rehhagel didn't speak Greek when he took the job. He learned it to connect with this players.

💬 23K   🔁 16K   ❤️ 60K   📊 26K   🔖 ⬆️

"We don't need stars. We need a system. And we need eleven players who will die for each other."

Nobody understood what he meant.

They were about to find out.

Shock Number One: Portugal Falls

June 12, 2004. Opening match.

Greece faced the host nation, Portugal. A team filled with stars like Luís Figo, Rui Costa, and a young Cristiano Ronaldo.

The Portuguese attacked. Greece absorbed the pressure like a sponge, then struck fast.

Giorgos Karagounis scored in the 7th minute. Angelos Basinas added another from the penalty spot.

Portugal pulled one back late through Cristiano Ronaldo, but it wasn't enough.

Final score: Greece 2, Portugal 1.

Suddenly, the football giants were paying attention.

Shock Number Two: France Goes Home

Quarter-finals. Lisbon. June 25, 2004.

Greece's next opponent: France, the defending European champions.

France had Zinedine Zidane, Thierry Henry, and Patrick Vieira. They were expected to cruise past the Greeks and continue their title defense.

The match was tense. France dominated possession. Zidane orchestrated attacks. Henry ran at defenders. But Greece's wall held firm.

Then, in the 65th minute, Charisteas rose above France's defense and powered a header into the net.

Greece 1, France 0.

When the final whistle blew, the world gasped.

The defending champions were going home early.

Shock Number Three: The Silver Goal

Semi-final. July 1, 2004. Against the Czech Republic.

The Czechs were the tournament's most exciting team.

Attacking football, flair, creativity. They'd beaten Germany and the Netherlands with ease.

For 90 minutes, Greece defended like their lives depended on it. The match went to extra time.

Then, in the 105th minute, defender Traianos Dellas headed the ball into the corner of the net.

GOAL.

The stadium erupted. Greece's players collapsed on the pitch, exhausted and disbelieving.

That goal became the last silver goal in a major international tournament. (Under the silver goal rule, if a team scored in the first period of extra time, the other team had until halftime of extra time to equalize. If they didn't, the match ended.)

Greece were in the final.

The Final:
Impossible Becomes Real

July 4, 2004. Estádio da Luz, Lisbon. The final.

Greece faced Portugal again. This time with over 60,000 Portuguese fans willing their team to victory.

For 56 minutes, Greece held firm. Then a corner kick swung into the box. Charisteas rose once more, timing his jump perfectly. A powerful header. The ball crashed into the net.

Greece 1, Portugal 0.

When the final whistle blew, Greece's players fell to their knees.

Otto Rehhagel stood on the sideline, tears streaming down his face. His system, built on discipline, trust, and unity, had defeated the richest, most talented teams in Europe.

In Athens, the streets erupted in celebration as if the whole country had declared a holiday. Car horns echoed through the night. Strangers hugged. Tears flowed. The Greek government held a national celebration.

Greece, the forgotten team, had become champions. Greece proved something bigger than football: Talent gets you noticed. Teamwork gets you trophies.

Eleven players who trusted each other more than they trusted fame. Eleven players who celebrated defensive blocks like they were goals. Eleven players who refused to believe that money and star power mattered more than heart.

Their success came from one simple idea: When everyone does their job, the impossible becomes possible.

THE BELIEVER

The alarm rang at five in the morning. The room was cold, the air thick with plaster dust. Ian Wright sat up, rubbed his eyes, and looked at his hands—rough, cracked, built for work, not for glory.

"Another day, mate," he muttered.

He ate a quick slice of toast, kissed his sleeping wife on the forehead, and stepped into the dark with his toolbox. By sunrise, he was knee-deep in cement, the radio humming football scores from the weekend. Every time a goal was mentioned, his trowel paused midair. *That should be me.*

Then he'd shake it off and keep working. But come Saturday, the plasterer turned into something else—a striker chasing a dream that refused to die.

In Brockley, South London, football had always been his escape. Life at home wasn't easy—Wright spent part of his childhood in care, moving between homes before finding stability. But on the pitch, everything made sense.

When other kids slept in, Wright was out kicking a flat ball against the wall until it split.

At school, his PE teacher—Mr. Pigden—saw something others didn't.

While Wright struggled in the classroom and faced challenges most kids his age didn't understand, Pigden became the steady presence he needed. Someone who believed in him when belief was hard to find.

"You've got something, Wrighty," Pigden told him more than once. "Don't waste it."

Those words stayed with Wright through every rejection that followed.

Chelsea said no.

Millwall said no.

Brighton said no.

WRIGHT'S PRESSING DRILL

Wright became famous for pressing defenders without giving up.

Here's how you can practice his relentless energy:

1. Pick a target (tree, cone, or friend with a ball)
2. Sprint toward them for 10 seconds at full speed
3. Rest for 30 seconds
4. Repeat 5 times

Wright's secret?

He imagined every sprint was his last chance to prove the doubters wrong.

What will YOU imagine when you're tired and want to quit?

By the time he was 21, most players his age were already pros with sponsorship deals and highlight reels. Wright was mixing cement and wondering if he'd missed his shot.

Then came a moment that could have ended everything. Wright was arrested for unpaid fines and spent a short time in custody. When he walked out, his mates laughed.

"You're 22, mate. Give it up. Get a real job."

But Wright had seen what giving up looked like. He refused to live there.

Wright worked by day, trained by night, and played whenever his legs still obeyed. He wasn't the biggest or the youngest. But he was the hungriest.

One muddy afternoon in 1985, playing in the Kent League (football's version of the forgotten leagues), Wright chased a loose ball like it was the World Cup final. The keeper rushed out. Wright chipped him with a grin, the ball floating over his head and dropping into the net.

A scout on the sideline scribbled something in his notebook. A week later, Crystal Palace called.

Wright thought it was a prank until he found himself in borrowed boots, scoring on his first day of training. At 21 years old, Ian Wright finally turned pro.

Most people would have been grateful and played it safe. Wright had bigger plans.

In 1991, Arsenal signed him for a record £2.5 million. Some fans groaned. "£2.5 million for a 28-year-old geezer from Palace?!"

Even teammates wondered if the boss had lost it. Wright heard every word.

Then he scored. And scored. And scored.

First game, first goal. Then another. Then 29 goals in his first season.

The chants of "Wright-y! Wright-y!" filled Highbury as he broke records, lifted trophies, and even scored on his England debut.

Can you believe Wright's first contract didn't involve money?

When Wright was signed by Crystal Palace from non-League club Greenwich Borough in 1985, the transfer fee was literally the club giving him weight-training gear.

By the time he retired, Wright had become Arsenal's all-time leading scorer—185 goals—and one of England's most dangerous strikers.

When he scored his record-breaking goal, he lifted his shirt to reveal a simple message: Just done it.

Wright once said, "I always believed, even when no one else did."

Here's what he learned that he wants YOU to know:

Belief isn't something you wait to feel. It's something you CHOOSE to do.

You do it when you're tired after training. You do it when someone says you're not good enough. You do it when the dream feels far away. And you keep doing it until you finally step into the place you've been holding in your mind.

Every "no" became fuel for the next "yes".

Think like Ian...

1. Wright worked as a plasterer while chasing his dream. What's something you're working toward even when it's hard?

2. Mr. Pidgen saw Wright's potential when others didn't. Who believes in YOU? How can you make them proud this week?

3. Wright heard "too old" and responded with 29 goals. When has someone doubted you? How did you respond—or how will you respond next time?

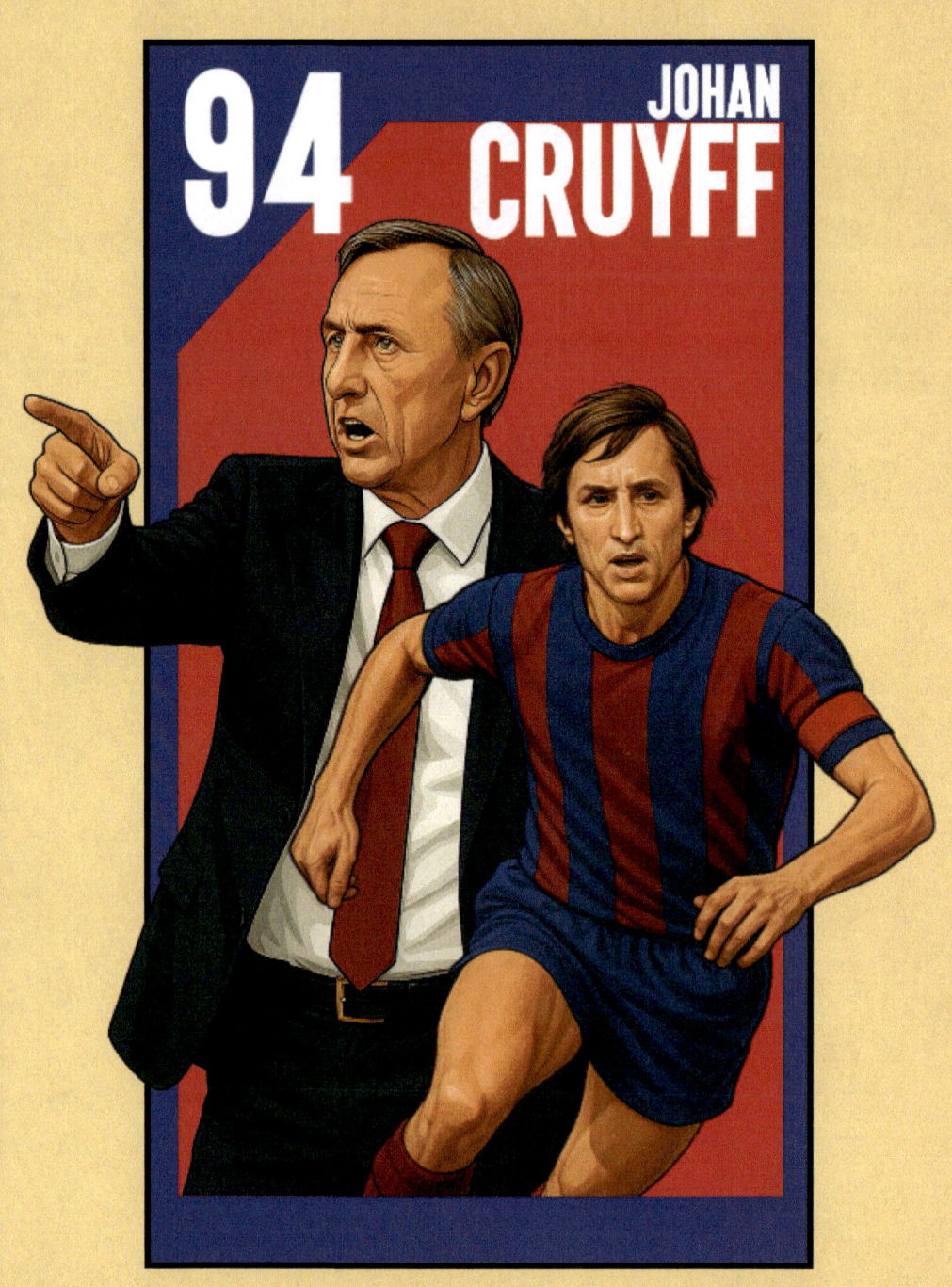

THE GAME CHANGER

Long before he stood on the touchline with a notepad in hand, Johan Cruyff was the kid from Amsterdam who saw football differently.

Growing up beside the Ajax stadium, he watched, learned, and dreamed. He wasn't the biggest or fastest, but he could see everything. The space before it opened. The pass before it was played. The pattern before it formed.

When he was ten, Ajax rejected him.

"Too frail," the scout said. "He won't survive against stronger boys."

His mother walked him back to the stadium the next day. And the next. And the next.

"Show them what you see," she whispered.

Johan saw patterns. Where the ball would bounce. Where teammates would run. Where gaps would open before they appeared.

He kept playing. Ajax kept watching.

By twelve, they signed him.

As a player, that vision made him a legend. Three European Cups with Ajax. A league title with Barcelona after fourteen barren years. And the 1974 World Cup, where his Netherlands side introduced Total Football, a dance of movement and intelligence that reshaped the game.

When his playing days ended, Cruyff became a coach. He taught teams to play the way he saw the game.

In 1988, Barcelona called him home as coach. The club was uncertain, searching for identity. The club had been struggling for years. The fans were angry. The board preferred safe, defensive football.

Some doubters whispered, "He's too different. This won't work."

Cruyff walked into the locker room with one belief:

"Playing football is simple. But playing simple football is the hardest thing there is."

He tore up the playbook. No long balls. No fear.

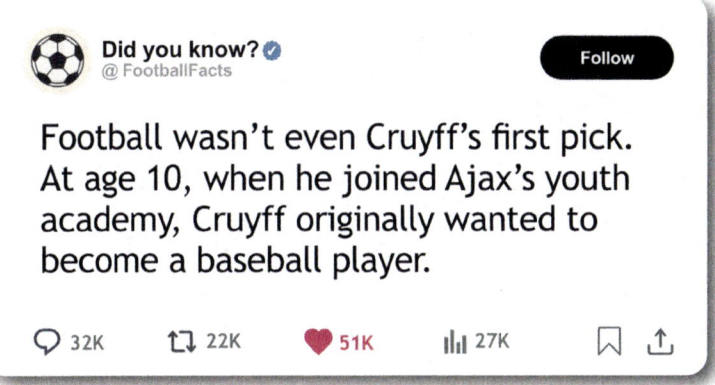

Did you know? ✔
@ FootballFacts

Follow

Football wasn't even Cruyff's first pick. At age 10, when he joined Ajax's youth academy, Cruyff originally wanted to become a baseball player.

💬 32K   🔁 22K   ❤️ 51K   📊 27K   🔖 ⬆️

Every player had to think, move, and trust the system: triangles, rhythm, possession.

Training became a classroom where mistakes were lessons.

"If you have the ball," he said, "the other team can't score."

It sounded obvious. It changed everything.

One defender complained, "But what if we lose the ball?"

Cruyff smiled. "Then you press immediately and win it back. Simple."

The players stared. They had never heard a coach talk like this.

By the early 1990s, his Dream Team came to life. Guardiola the conductor. Laudrup the artist. Stoichkov the spark.

They won four straight La Liga titles and Barcelona's first European Cup in 1992.

But trophies were only part of the story. Cruyff was planting a philosophy that would outlive him.

He reimagined La Masia's philosophy, shaping how young players were taught to think, not just play.

Years later, Messi, Xavi, and Iniesta would carry those ideas onto the world stage.

Guardiola, his student, summed it up: "Everything I know, I learned from Johan."

Cruyff coached like he played. Brave. Curious. Unafraid to be different.

CRUYFF BY THE NUMBERS

- **3 European Cups** as a player (Ajax, 1971-73)

- **14 years** since Barcelona's last league title when he arrived as coach

- **4 straight La Liga titles** with the Dream Team (1991-94)

- **1992** - Barcelona's first European Cup in club history

- **33 goals** in **48 games** for Netherlands

- **Age 41** when he became Barcelona coach

"You play football with your head," he told his teams, "and your legs follow."

Every short pass, every patient build-up, from Spain's tiki-taka to Guardiola's Manchester City, traces back to Cruyff's sketches and his belief in simplicity.

Even now, when a kid stops, spins, and makes a defender chase shadows, they're using the famous

Cruyff Turn, a move he invented in the 1974 World Cup that still fools defenders today.

The Mastermind 🤯

> Johan Cruyff helped shape the Total Football philosophy — a system where every player could switch positions and play anywhere on the pitch.

Cruyff showed the world that football is a game you play with your brain first. He taught players to ask, "Where's the space?" before asking, "Where's the ball?"

His ideas live on every time a team keeps the ball, moves as a unit, and thinks two passes ahead.

Your turn: Next time you play, try this: Before you get the ball, look around. Where's the empty space? Where will you pass BEFORE you even touch it?

That's thinking like Cruyff.

What will you see that others miss?

THE CRUYFF TRIANGLE DRILL

You'll need: *2 friends, 1 ball*

The Challenge:

1. Stand in a triangle, 5 meters apart
2. Pass the ball using ONLY 2 touches
3. After you pass, move to a NEW spot
4. Keep the triangle shape but keep moving

Goal:

20 passes without the ball stopping

Why it works:

Cruyff believed in "triangles" because they create passing options. This drill teaches you to think AND move at the same time.

Cruyff's Secret:

"The ball moves faster than you can run. So pass it, then move to where you're needed next."

FOREVER YOUNG

The first sound Kazu remembers wasn't a lullaby, but the soft thump of a football in the narrow yard outside his home in Shizuoka.

Football wasn't something he learned to love, it was simply always there. His uncle coached, his brother played and by the time he was six, Kazu was already copying the older boys' tricks just to fit in.

By fourteen, Kazu was the best in his district. But Japan had no professional league yet. If he wanted to become a footballer, he had to leave.

He watched videos of Brazilian players and saw something different. They didn't just play football. They danced with it.

At fifteen, he did what no one in Japan had done before. He packed a single bag and flew to Brazil, chasing the game at its source.

The first week, three clubs said no.

One coach laughed: "Go home, kid. Brazil is for Brazilians."

Kazu didn't speak enough Portuguese to argue.

So he showed them with his feet instead.

Remember Miura's words:

"As long as the ball rolls, so will I."

He trained through the heat. Through the loneliness. Through the speed of Brazilian football that made everything back home feel slow. Some nights he called his family, homesick and exhausted. Some mornings he woke up wondering if he'd made a mistake.

But every time he touched the ball, something shifted. Joy became his fuel.

By nineteen, he was playing for Santos FC—the same club where Pelé once danced with the ball.

When Kazu returned to Japan in the early 1990s, football was still finding its voice. Then came the J.League—and with it, King Kazu.

In 1993, he scored twenty goals, won MVP, and led Verdy Kawasaki to back-to-back titles.

A year later, he became the first Japanese player to score in Italy's Serie A.

As captain of his national team and Asian Player of the Year, he helped Japan believe it belonged on the world stage.

Stadiums chanted his name. Kids wore his number. But Kazu never stopped working.

Most players retire when their legs slow down.

Kazu's legs are slower now—but his hunger hasn't faded.

At fifty-eight, he still beats teenagers to training. He still studies every pass. He still celebrates goals like he's seventeen.

In 2023, he became the oldest professional footballer in history. When teammates half his age complain about a tough session, Kazu just smiles and runs another sprint.

When reporters ask why he doesn't retire, he grins:

"Because the ball still wants to play."

For Kazu, football was never something to finish.

It's something to become.

He didn't chase records or retirement plans. He chased the feeling that he had at six years old in that narrow yard in Shizuoka.

Here's what Kazu would ask you:

What's the thing you love so much you'd do it even when it gets hard? Even when you're the oldest in the room? Even when no one's watching?

FUN FACT ZONE

Miura's trademark celebration is the "Kazu Dance," a joyful routine he performs every time he scores — and yes, he's still doing it in his fifties!

Miura scored at 50 years and 14 days, becoming the oldest player ever to score in a professional league match.

THE SUCCESS STORY

Blue banners soared as the whistle blew at King Power Stadium. This wasn't just another match. It was the final act of a fairy tale. A city had woken. A team had dared.

In August 2015, no one gave Leicester a chance. No stars, no billionaire owners, just fighters in blue. Nobody believed in them. The betting odds said they had a better chance of being abducted by aliens than winning the league.

The previous season, they had barely survived relegation, finishing 14th with 41 points after being bottom in April. Pundits predicted they'd be back in the Championship by Christmas. One newspaper headline read: "Leicester City: Doomed."

One of their leaders, Esteban Cambiasso, had left for another club. Their squad was valued at roughly £60 million — less than Chelsea's bench that season.

Then Claudio Ranieri arrived as manager, part teacher, part dreamer. Critics mocked the hiring. "The Tinkerman," they called him, remembering his struggles at Greece and Chelsea. Sports writers questioned whether he was "past it."

But Ranieri had learned from every setback. "If your attitude isn't 100 percent," he warned his players, "I get crazy." He didn't promise trophies, only belief.

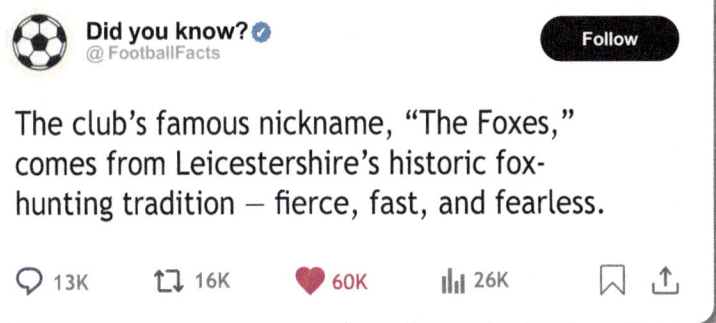

Did you know? ✓
@ FootballFacts

Follow

The club's famous nickname, "The Foxes," comes from Leicestershire's historic fox-hunting tradition — fierce, fast, and fearless.

💬 13K   🔁 16K   ❤️ 60K   📊 26K   🔖 ↥

Leicester didn't try to outplay the giants. They pressed, countered, and struck like lightning. "I'm not a magician," Ranieri smiled. "I'm a normal man who works with passion, with love."

Slowly, the heartbeat of the city began to match the rhythm of the team.

The Spark

The first spark came in September 2015. Two goals down against Aston Villa, Leicester came back to win 3–2. A match that turned hope into belief.

By November, Jamie Vardy was rewriting records, scoring in eleven straight Premier League games. From a factory worker to a record-breaker, he just laughed: "I just hit it."

Soon after, Riyad Mahrez danced through defenders, scoring a hat-trick at Swansea and helping Leicester reach the top of the table. The question echoed across England: Could they actually do it?

The Turning Point

February 2016 became the moment everything changed. Under the Anfield floodlights, Vardy volleyed from 25 yards. A goal that felt like destiny taking shape. Liverpool 0, Leicester 2.

A week later, Leicester stunned Manchester City 3–1 at the Etihad. The team everyone expected to fade was pulling away. The whispers were gone. Belief had taken over.

The Final Push

Spring arrived tense and electric. 1–0 at Watford. 1–0 at Crystal Palace. 1–0 against Southampton. Narrow wins built on grit and heart.

Ranieri joked after one match, "We keep giving away goals! I tell them, this is not possible!" So they stopped. The defense became a wall.

When Shinji Okazaki's bicycle kick hit the net against Newcastle, the roar was so loud it registered as a minor earthquake on monitoring equipment nearby.

The Night it Happened

By May, Leicester had played their last match. Now they could only wait and watch.

Their rivals Tottenham were still chasing them. If Tottenham won their remaining matches, they could still steal the title. But tonight, Tottenham faced Chelsea. If Chelsea could stop them from winning, Leicester would be champions.

Across the city, fans gathered around TVs. Players watched from homes and restaurants. The whole city held its breath.

Spurs struck twice in the first half. 2–0. Leicester's dream was slipping away. Then, in the 83rd minute, Hazard picked up the ballnear halfway.

"Hazard driving forward… one defender beaten… two."

He struck.

"HAZARD! Oh, what a goal! 2–1!"

But it wasn't enough. Leicester needed Tottenham NOT to win.

Minutes crawled by. Tottenham pushed forward, desperate. Then, in stoppage time, Hazard got the ball again.

"Hazard once more… he's through… GOAL!"

The referee blew three sharp blasts. Full-time: 2–2.

Tottenham had dropped points. The math was done.

Leicester were champions.

Fireworks crackled across the sky. Car horns blared through every street. Strangers hugged each other. The impossible had happened.

Ranieri laughed through tears: "Dilly ding, dilly dong! We are in the Champions League, man!"

Five days later, under blue confetti at the King Power Stadium, Morgan lifted the Premier League trophy. Andrea Bocelli sang, fans wept and the impossible became real.

Ranieri stood beside his captain, clapping softly. "The best player," he said, "was the team."

What They Taught the World

Leicester City proved that chemistry beats cash, that belief can outlast talent, and that ordinary people can achieve extraordinary things when they refuse to accept what's "impossible."

They didn't have the best players. They had the best team. They didn't have the most money. They had the most heart.

They didn't listen to the odds.

They made their own.

LEICESTER TEAM DRILL

Leicester's secret?

They celebrated defensive blocks like goals.

Try this at practice:

- When a teammate makes a great tackle or block, the WHOLE team sprints to congratulate them
- Count clean sheets and defensive stops just like you count goals
- Create an "unsung hero" award each match for the player who worked hardest off the ball

Why it works:

When everyone feels valued, everyone fights harder. Leicester's defense was as important as their attack.

This is not the end. It's just the kick-off for YOUR career! ⚽🌐

Grab a ball, get outside, and start practicing. Maybe one day I'll be writing a book about YOU! 👊🌟

Remember... Dream big, work hard and never let the final whistle blow on your dreams! 🏆🔥

Did you know? ✔
@ FootballFacts

Scan Me!

Don't wait for the highlights. Give us your post-match analysis and leave a review on Amazon!

💬 13K   ↻ 16K   ❤ 60K   📊 26K   🔖 ⬆

You made it to the end of the book!

Every single person you read about started exactly like you: a kid with a dream. Some were doubted. Some made big mistakes. Some failed more times than they could count.

But they kept going no matter how hard it got.

If there's one lesson you take from this book, let it be that. Now it's your turn.

<u>Think about the story that stood out to you.</u>

When life gets tough, remember what your hero did... and show yourself that you can do it too. Football, like life, should be fun. No matter what happens, what obstacles or challenges show up, you can choose how you respond to any situation.

Be proud of the small wins, learn from hard moments and keep getting up no matter how many times you fall. You've got this champ!

Printed in Dunstable, United Kingdom

75115347R00067